Dancing With the Beloved

Dancing With the Beloved

The Selected Words of Muhammad-I-Hafiz-I-Shiraz (from the *Divan*)

Translated from the Persian by

Thomas Rain Crowe

Companions for the Journey Volume 33

WHITE PINE PRESS / BUFFALO, NEW YORK

White Pine Press
P.O. Box 236
Buffalo, NY 14201
www.whitepine.org

Publication of this book was supported by public funds from the New York State Council on the Arts, with the support of Governor Kathy Hochul and the New York State Legislature, a State Agency.

Book Design: Elaine LaMattina:

Printed and bound in the United States of America.

ISBN 978-1-945680-92-2

Library of Congress Control Number: 2026934352

CONTENTS

PREFACE

The poems of Muhammad-I-Hafiz-I-Sharaz were composed during the 14th century in Persia. Hafiz, in the tradition of previous and later Sufi Masters, established a literary tradition of hope, love, joy, thanksgiving, and universal harmony. Hafiz was highly celebrated in his own day and much in demand and active in the courts and in the streets throughout the Middle East. He is said to have received his poetic gifts from the prophet Elijah who gave him a drink of the waters-of-life. He then traveled around Persia reciting his poems, which were written down by his students and scribes in the language of the common man. In much of the Islamic world, Hafiz is considered to be one of the greatest poets of all time. Since his death around 1389, his legendary status has continued down through the centuries, inspiring praise from Western literary luminaries such as Goethe, Emerson, Lorca, and spiritual masters such as Meher Baba, who said of Hafiz, "There is no equal to Hafiz in poetry. His *Divan* is the best book in the world because it engenders feelings which ultimately lead to illumination."

Not fluent in Farsi, I couldn't do literal translations of Hafiz's poems from that linguistic source, but could do versions or "trans-renderings" of scholarly but outdated English translations from the Farsi that were done back in the 1800s and early 1900s by a number of people, including, primarily, Wilberforce Clarke. My intent was to try and get the best interpretations for a more modern English language version of Hafiz's work, which I did in two previous publications (1998 and 2001) that have reached wide and diverse audiences both here in the U.S. and abroad. Going back over both of those collections after many years, I marked and chose favorite lines and couplets from the ghazals and created a kind of "best of" or "selected words" for this Hafiz volume. In most cases these entries won't be complete poems from the previous collections but combined mix-and-match mini-versions focusing on certain metaphors, segments, or spiritual insights which Hafiz wanted to emphasize in his attempt to raise human consciousness to a level of true spirituality and social sustainability. Chief among these recurring symbolic images are "the rose," "wind," "garden," "ocean," "the door," "pearl," and various endearing names for God. Taken from Hafiz's complete collection in *The Divan,* I have gathered here couplets and lines, most of which orbit around the subject of "wine," a metaphor for God's love. In Hafiz's Street of the Divine lives God the Wineseller, who is the source of all of Hafiz's spiritually romantic longing.

In my versioning of these poem sections from *The Divan* that are from more literal and academic translations done during the previous two centuries, I have tried to be true to the "folk" and/or peasant sensibilities which I believe to be inherent in the original Persian. My process consisted in taking the scholarship of Wilberforce Clarke and trying to create a believable blend of fourteenth-century Islamic spirituality and twenty-first century American sensibility to create a bridge to our own century and to bring an engaging yet valid voice to the English-speaking world. Somewhat like the Welsh language poets of the European peasant "Praise" tradition, these poems, not unlike Shakespeare's plays, are written for the common man in common everyday speech as seen through eyes that don't idolize individualism and separation. Rather, they reflect the human potential of living in a world of harmony and grace. During a time of international political and religious chaos and violence, perhaps this work will in some way be an essential guide for our survival and recovery. Always the humble teacher, Hafiz, the Perfect Master, sits with us on the barstool in the town pub like a mirror, reflecting back our dreams.

—Thomas Rain Crowe

I.
In the Street of the Divine

Winebringer! More wine!
Keep my glass full, forever fresh and new.

When will you ever enjoy the fruits-of-life
if you don't drink wine?
A toast to the Beloved! Forever fresh and new.

The messenger who came from the land of the Master,
brought my life's destiny, written in His hand.

It is thanks to God, and God alone, that his
fee and my message cost the same.

If not in body, perhaps I will see my Beloved in sleep.
Sweet words that stir the heart and mind are a gift from God!

I am just a winedrinker—head spinning and looking for love.
With cup in hand,
the Beloved one day walked into the Winehouse.
And with only a wink
intoxicated all those already drunk with wine.
When He got up to leave,
the hearts of those in the Winehouse sank.
When He sat back down, the cheer that went up was deafening.
Those dark eyes and long eyelashes
seduce whoever is touched by their glance.

I am my own worst enemy,
yet the wine-drenched love I have for God, is my only affair.

Gardener, don't chase me from Your garden like the wind.
These red, rare tears of mine are water for Your fruit.

Whoever taught Hafiz to write these poems, softly,
has the voice of a nightingale in love, and is, for life, my friend.

✡

O wind, if you are going past the rosebed of the Beloved,
please take this message:
"Why have you taken our names from Your memory book?
Winter is coming, and like the tulip
my heart is closing from the cold.
O Bird of Paradise, when will you come again to our cage?"

In the eyes of the Beloved that have stolen our hearts
is the best drink!
In the blue green sea of sky, the crescent moon floats like a boat,
yet is drowned in the gaze of the Beloved.

Hafiz, keep on dropping the grain of tears from Your eyes,
it could be the Bird of Union that takes our bait one night!

✡

My mad heart has a secret
that no one knows.

The Beloved has stolen even the sweet solitude from my heart,
and I am content.

No one who has ever laid eyes on this silver-limbed Cypress
would ever go looking in the woods for a cypress again.

"Hafiz," the voice of inner wine will say;
"Be careful what you ask for,
you may just get what you want one day."

✲

The beautiful face of the Beloved doesn't need
makeup, eyeliner, perfume or our imperfect love.

I know for a fact that the beauty of Joseph, growing daily,
brought out from behind the veil the beauty of Mary, too.

O, young people, listen to this good advice:
cherish the teachings of the wise old Masters
even more than the voice of your heart.

Let's drink good wine and sing great songs
instead of talking about destiny.
Reason can't fit into that full glass,
or between the notes of that song.

Listening to this ghazal of Hafiz is like stringing pearls;
sing it sweetly, and wear that song like stars!

✡

From the fields where the breeze of Paradise blows,
drink, forever, that wine.

O fanatics and pious wise ones,
guzzle your wine and pray!

If you are looking for the Fountain of Youth,
gaze into your wineglass, and listen for the sound of the harp.

Just like the face of the Winebringer is promise of more wine,
promise to drink wine in rose season.

Hafiz, do not worry and grieve;
at the end of the wedding the Bride of Fortune will lift
her veil, and you can look into her shining face!

✡

O pilgrim, listen to the nightingale!
How happy it is united with the rose.
It's loving song can be heard only while walking in Your field.

O Beloved, cure our sick hearts with Your healing kiss.
Heal us with a dose of Your wine.

Even in service, my body is unworthy of You;
and my soul, merely dust on your doorstep.

What a horseman you are!
So good that the wild colt obeys You.

Here is what I think:
The music of Your party is loud and goes on all night long.
The poems of Hafiz are only two notes in that tune.

✲

The Winebringer has poured into my cup a wine of many colors.
In this one glass alone I can see the image of all creation.

The Magician who knows that this world is just a trick
of illusion has packed up all His equipment
and keeps quiet about the whole affair.

These days, the only friend that is faultless
is a bottle of red wine and a book of poems.

In this noisy street, the voice of reason says:
the world and all its possessions is no security.

Everything you see around you will one day disappear,
except Love, which lasts forever.

Now that I have raised the glass of pure wine to my lips,
the nightingale starts to sing!

Break all your ties with people who profess to teach,
and learn from the Pure Bird.
From Pole to Pole,
the news of those sitting in quiet solitude is spreading.

It's not important whether we drink Gallo or Mouton Cadet,
drink up!
And be happy, for whatever our Windebringer brings,

is the essence of grace.

Everyone, sober or drunk, is in his own way, seeking the Beloved.
Whether mosque, church, or a stand of trees,
everywhere is a place of prayer.

✡

Here in the Winehouse, we are not hypocrites, drunk on deceit.
He who knows our hearts will attest to this in a court of law.

We carry out the commandments of God and don't hurt anyone,
and whatever we are told is "unlawful," we don't twist to make it "law."

What good is this talking of "laws" when
with your lips, of the Divine Order you do partake?

From now on, I promise to make idleness a spiritual retreat.
My path is that of drunkenness and my street is the Street of Love.

Don't worry, be happy! with what you have this moment.
The treasures of the heart are not found on land or at sea.

Happiness is: a river's bank, the shade of a willow,
and the poetic mind of a friend.
To the bride-of-nature I give all my fantasies
of virgins at night in my bed.

Know that even one night spent with the Beloved is a great gift.
Be happy, for the moon is shining, your heart's on fire,
and the river is low in its banks.

O, Hafiz, the Water-of-Life is full of mud because of your poems.
No one has ever written words like this out of the desire for Love

✲

Friend, get up!
How long will you sit there in the door of the college?
Get up! You must be dreaming. This is not the Winehouse door!

And friends, do not think less of Hafiz
for looking lustfully at beautiful women.
I love you too. When I look at women this way,
I see only lovers of God.

Since I have taken the path of devotion to the Beloved,
I have the power to make a hundred beggars rich,
and a pauper of the king.

O Beloved, be benevolent so that at least I can continue to write.
I pray every day to Your beauty, and I am filled with grace!

✡

I get all my prophecy from today's good cheer.
Meanwhile, I pray that my Lord
of mountains and streams does hear.

Today, I make a prayer for all the Winesellers, and why shouldn't I?
To return the kindness and free drinks of such a generous host.

Even though Hafiz is dead drunk and half crazy,
his face is lit up and his body alive
with the hope and grace of the Beloved!

✡

O, Beloved, because You are the candle of every gathering,
it is me that is consumed by light.
Don't look away. I can't bear the absence of Your stare.

If Your Love is like the thunder and lightning in the sky,
it will kill Hafiz.
So, be gentle, I am a frail servant who only wants to love
his life, and live!

The only way to be pure of heart is by being a lover.
With these wet mirrors of mine, how can I see Your face?

In this swollen river, I clutch the boat of Hafiz's *Divan.*
All I've got now to keep me afloat are words.

Whether I'm a drunk or a Perfect Master,
my secret is that I am only Hafiz.
He who writes poetry must also love his wine!

✲

On the blackboard of the heart,
I have straight A's in my love for the Beloved.
Meanwhile, my eyes pour out the blood of my heart.

Listen to what my pen has to say: for this drop of ink
is worth more than all the shining jewels you own.

Hafiz, I've never seen or heard poems more beautiful than yours,
which, like the Koran, you hold tight and close to your heart.

☆

Professor, you give such strange advice
from your books that say: "Don't try love."
I say: there is no expert in the name of Love.

The soul of the man with a heart is alive with love!
If you don't have love,
you're excused from this class—now go away!

Hafiz, you cannot tell everyone the secret of the heart
so they'll understand;
but tell those who have suffered distance from the Beloved
and they will understand your song!

✲

Listen to what Hafiz has to say: Stay away from the bad
and work toward the good.
Do not play games or toy with life or it will rot.

Surrender yourself to the Beloved!
Don't sit around waiting for help.
Surrender is like a loud voice that the Winebringer hears
over all his other customers.
And He will bring you all the wine you need.

✡

If, from hate, your friend cuts you with his knife;
like the bountiful mine, give him gold.

O, Seeker, I have come from Paradise to bring you some happy news!
Amidst my sweet songs, my raucous jokes, and my beautiful stories,
I say, "Put on a feast that costs you everything you have,
in honor of the real King of wealth. And give it all away!"

☆

O, blessed Bird, come again and sing to me of better days;
of the past, and of the future to which we will return.

O, friends, you are living in the Garden of Eden, so have fun!
God is not keeping score of every misdeed you have done.

O, Winebringer, there will never be a better day for happiness.
O, Hafiz, have another glass of wine!
Today is all the time you need.

✡

For many years now, I have been caretaker of the Winehouse.
and have resigned myself to that job for the rest of my life.

What kind of armour can you use against the arrows of destiny?
Can you stop Fate with a spear or a shield?

Hafiz says, "Look into the dust of the crystal ball
and see the nature of time.
Now, fold up your carpets of desire and tear in two your pages of
indulgent poems, and follow the Path that to the Beloved, comes.

This is the road that leads to the Winehouse.
It is for those seeking and those listening,
not for the blind, deaf, and dumb."

✡

This morning, because of all my grief, while writing poetry,
my words revolted and ran away...

They ran, complaining, past the shrines of Rumi and Kabir,
and through the land of Solomon, and kept going...

They ran along the banks of the sacred river,
and by the palace of the king, and kept on going...

They ran past the house of the One who, alone,
understands the soul of language, and kept on going...

I called out to my soul: "Old friend, where are you going?"
Its heartsick and weeping reply was angry and harsh,
and it kept on going...

I shouted louder: "O Words, will you never speak to me again
in sweet rhymes?"
But the sweet words and the sweet verses only ran faster,
kept going...

I pleaded: "Do not go!" But they turned a deaf ear,
Like that of the king or the chancellor
who is too busy to be bothered with the lovers of wine.

O, Perfect Master, please call back these words of mine
that have gotten away. What is a man like Hafiz, on fire, to do?

Who with love overflowing, and no words,
has nothing more to say.

✡

II.
The Ocean of Love

The Ocean of Love is a sea where there is no shore;
and without the soul's surrender, there is no hope, no sand.

I lay my head, each night, in submission on the bricks
at the Winehouse door.
If You are caressing my wish,
I will not turn my back on the world.

Hafiz pays no attention to the censors and the critics.
Writing poems full of love, beyond reason, is his one desire.

✡

The beauty of this poem is beyond words.
Do you need a guide to experience the heat of the sun?

Blessed is the brush of the painter who paints
such beautiful pictures for his virgin bride.

Look at this beauty. There is no reason for what you see.
Experience its grace. Even in nature there is nothing so fine.

Either this poem is a miracle, or some sort of magic trick,
guided either by Gabriel or the Invisible Voice, inside.

No one, not even Hafiz, can describe with words the Great Mystery.
No one knows in which shell the priceless pearl does hide.

✲

O, pilgrim, there is something that I want to say:
since your glass of wine is full, share it with others,
that, they, too, may taste the love of God.
Together, all of us here are hoping to see His face.

To you, young one, I say take my advice and keep silent
so that you will become old and wise before your time.

No rosary or holy coat can give you the high of being drunk;
so go to the Wineseller. He will give you all the help you need.

But be careful, for Satan will tempt you at every turn:
he is everywhere,
so be silent and listen for the advice of angels and your heart.

So, lets bring out the harp and beat loudly on the drum.
Hafiz may be drunk,
but he will never soil Your flowing gown of gold.

✲

Winebringer, come quick!
For the Beloved has taken off His veil.
O, Beloved, now that you are here, under the sun and moon,
work has taken a new meaning.

The radios of the seven heavens
are playing this story over the air waves,
while those with small ears
listen to stations only playing silly songs.

Hafiz, where did you learn the magic of writing words?
The Beloved seems to have turned your weary wail into gold!

✲

Like the morning breeze,
if you bring to the morning good deeds,
the rose of your desire will open and bloom.

Go forward, and make advances down this road of Love,
and like a laughing candle,
you can abandon the life you live in your head.

Hafiz, if you are listening to this good advice,
the road of Love and its enrichment are right around the curve.

✡

Good news! These hard times won't last forever.
Good times and bad times are both the same, neither lasts.

O, candle, attracting the moth is not a cause for grief.
Celebrate this union,
for dawn and the end to self-reflection are near.

No matter what the future brings, why be happy or sad,
for even on the pages of the Book of Life
the writing will someday fade.

On the dome of this Winehouse it has been written in gold:
"We only accept credit cards made from plastic of pure hearts."

This morning, there was more good news:
permission to unite with Him.
The message said: "Caught in grief's cage, surrender is your reward."

Hafiz, don't ever stop longing for the wine of the Beloved;
His goodness will wash all this tyranny and violence away!

✲

Since you have promised me union,
what is there left here for me to do?

As your lover, all I've ever asked for is a glance.
Even one breath from the Beloved would be enough.

Good wine is good company, and so is the Beloved.
Hafiz has lost his heart to this union and will always be this way.

✡

O Winebringer, throw some of Your best wine in our face,
for it is time to wake up!

Today, reason is the currency of the world,
but compared with Love, even alchemy has lost its flash.

To a millionaire, money is the standard of the world.
Hafiz says: O beggars,
I have exchanged all my money for these poems!

*

O Beloved, we know that by breaking in love's door,
we are bound to karma.
Think about tomorrow—it's better to mix something sour
with what is sweet.

So, drink up! Drink everything you have.
And don't worry, death's sword is dull today.

Remember: wine charms reason's wits and takes its rust away.
This vineyard will be here from now to Judgement Day!

Hafiz, you chose the path to the Winehouse, happily;
so from this path of prayer and love, don't stray.

✡

O, Winebringer, this cup of wine is like Christ,
by its very nature it can raise the dead.

O, Minstrel, play something beautiful, so that I will
want to dance like Jupiter and all the stars!

O, Master, where do You get all these pearls?
Pilgrim, put down that book you are reading
about money and the rich.

Hafiz says: Look for wealth in the Sea of Love,
not in the Book of Desire.
Only by swimming naked and diving
will you become purified in pearls!

*

Hafiz says: "Come here, all of you who are like me,
and let's celebrate our good fortune.
Along the Path, whatever befalls the traveler is for his own good.
It is impossible to lose your way on a straight stretch of road.

What is this room we're in, full of clouds and sky?
To this question there are no answers
and no sage who knows the way.

Master, why have You given us the power of free will?
For all its potential, all it does is make us cry.

So, if you have something to say, speak up!
Don't be shy. In this courtroom there is no jury and no judge.

What does it matter that Hafiz does not sit on some lofty throne?
He sits all day in the Winehouse and drinks the dregs—
and for this they have made him king!

☆

Hafiz, if you have had enough of this world and all its violence,
then take up the cup;
and from the inside let this liquid love make peace.

These days, the only friend that is faultless
is a bottle of red wine and a book of poems.

I am not the only writer that is worried about having a job.
Knowledge without experience is the "wise man's" fate.

Everything you see around you will one day disappear,
except Love, which lasts forever.

I say hold on to the Moon-Faced One's hair, and don't tell a soul!
For the effect of Saturn and the stars, is agony and good luck.

No one will ever see Hafiz sober, never.
He is drunk on the wine of endless Eternity,
and keeps asking for more!

✡

That moon-eyed girl has stolen my heart again!
But now I'm weeping with a heart full of tears.

And all this after I'd spent a small fortune on her
for expensive silks and cloth,just to be close to her moonlike face.

I guess I should be thankful for the company of an angel
rather than being stuck in the Winehouse
with all those sweating men!

O, gypsy girl, have pity on this beggar and wino at your door.
I have given up everything I have. For you!

Say something. Anything hot and sexy will do;
but please, throw no more water on these flames!

Come here! Last night I dreamed I was content
and this surely must have something to do with you!

You and I were destined to be as one,
for it is written in the Book of Dreams.

When I die, tie a cup on my coffin, so that
when I rise from the dead I can quench my thirst with wine.

Hafiz, get up, and run to the Beloved before this goes too far.
Don't be like that silly rabbit who built his lover's likeness out of tar!

☆

Even though there is darkness within,
from Beyond a lamp can light up the cell of a monk.

He who throws himself at the Beloved's feet
is like a workhorse and will be rewarded
with boundless pastures and eternal rest.

I will spare you from my speech about reason and books,
and let you hear it from the harp and the lute, who tell it best.

Yet, only great poems
can capture the hearts of those who don't read.
So poets, sing! Let the God-of-Oceans
fill your mouths with pearls.

O, Hafiz, if you are seeking the pearl of union, do this:
from tears, make yourself an ocean and then dive!

✡

To all you restless roses
who have given your power away to thorns,
I say: "A nightingale would never give its voice away to crows!

So, if you are tired and hot, don't go looking for shade
beneath the Tree of Life or beneath the lotus!
There is no cool breeze unless you know the Truth.

And I say to the professors:
"Be careful and don't always think you are right.
For the distance from the monk's cell to the Master's abode
is less than you think."

So, if it is fame and glory that you are looking for from the sun,
then go back to sleep, there is only divine knowledge in its rays.

Because of the blessing and the magic of the sun and moon,
I have been free of the illness of fate and time.

If it is fame and fortune you desire
that seems always just out of reach,
try and change that if you can, but remember destiny.

If your life has hit hard times,
go to the Winehouse and enjoy some wine.
This elixir can turn even a beggar's meager fortune into gold.
Hafiz, for now at least, rejoice—then scatter the sugar of thanks.

With sweet wine on your lips,
you have drunk fully of this life, and how sweet it is!

☆

Even though generosity is only a word whose origin cannot
be traced, go ahead and give what you have
to those who are hungry and in need.

Not everyone who writes verses is a poet
and is welcomed with applause.
But in this world of illustrious birds,
I am a poor falcon and have learned to fly fast!

From my pen, listen to the mysteries of love and wine.
For each night you'll find Hafiz drinking
with the Pleiades and the moon.

✡

O Beloved, tell us of divine knowledge and the life of the heart
before we tear off the roof of the sky
and go out on the wrong path.

Minstrel, since you've got your harp in your hand,
sing us a song of love so we can dance, waving hands,
as we make our way down the dance line.

While one person boasts of reason,
another speaks of inspired trance.
Come, let's take this discourse to God and let Him be the judge.

With my wineglass in my hand,
I am far away from judges and righteous saints.
I only hang out, here in the Winehouse, with the pure of heart.

But don't worry, I'm only a servant of the Master of the Age.
If I had any real sense, I'd go searching for relief on High.

Almost nowhere now
do they appreciate the art of poetry and spiritual talk.
Hafiz says: "Don't worry,
to somewhere else that is rich with freedom we will go."

✡

Here in Shiraz,
every night my love-sick cry is the first one you will hear.
If you added my tears to the Zinda River,
all the farmlands in Iraq would be washed away by flood.

I went after the Beloved with a passion, my lips ready for a kiss,
but he put me off, saying: "I've got a headache,
and it's bad luck to make love on a waning moon."

O Sufi, to sit and watch the dervishes won't do you any harm.
Even Solomon the Great found pleasure in watching ants.

Hafiz, it's not a virus or the flu that has made you feel this way;
you are wine-sick, and the only cure for you is wine.

✡

Last night the message was sent out from the Winehouse:
"All sins have been pardoned, so drink all the wine you need!"

We should have known all along that the grace of God
is greater than silence or all our sins combined.

My head is tangled in the curls of the Beloved's hair,
and my face is covered in Winehouse dust.

Hafiz says: "Even though the pious say my drinking is a sin,
I know this isn't so—I was born thirsty, and this wine
is a gift from God!

✲

Last night a nightingale came to my window and sang.
Its song was so sweet I listened, and it had this to say:
"If spiritual enlightenment is taking too long
and you are tired of the world,
then give up everything, even your words."

Even if waves of misfortune were to come
crashing on the roof of the sky,
the poor and pure of heart would stay completely dry.

O Beloved, when I drink from Your red glass,
I lose consciousness.
When I look into Your drunken eyes, I go deaf.

Everywhere I go, I carry a wine cask on my shoulder,
hoping that someone will give me, in exchange, Your cup.

Don't tell me to meditate
or try to hold my breath to remedy my pain.
Would the bird in the meadow take such ill advice?

So lovers of wine, drink up! The Beloved has lifted his red glass
and Paradise cannot be, now, far away.

✲

This morning I went into the rose garden.
The nightingale's song was so sweet
that the narcissus began to cry, and the tulip
drank the narcissus's tears in passion and in pain.

To show her disapproval,
the lily stuck out her tongue like a sword,
and, like a bigamist's wife, the anemone opened up her mouth
to tell the world of her travails.

Hafiz, learn from the flowers and the Gardener
the difference between pleasure and joy.
And remember: there would be no messenger if there had
been no message sent today.

✡

Even if everyone in all God's creation forbids me love,
I'll do whatever my Beloved wishes, whatever that may be.

He who sits in the center of the Sufi's circle
sits in hope that his sitting will gain blessings from the Beloved.

With clean air, beautiful scenery, and good wine,
all that's needed for perfection is a joyous heart.

The earth will never be without flowers and trees.
For as one dies, another comes to take its place.

O beggar, don't ask me what you should do. Look inside.
This mirror will tell you all you need to know.

To the moon-eyed girl, I said: "Come on, give us a little kiss.
Your sweet lips will save me from a broken heart."

She only laughed: "Hafiz, I am not afraid of your kiss,
but turn your lips instead to the face of the Beloved!"

☆

If the sun is the wine and the moon is the cup,
then pour some of that sun into my mooncup
and let's cause an eclipse!

The reason-mongers say that being a wine addict
is either right or wrong.
Winebringer, I don't care what they say. bring me some more wine!

Although I'm already a little tipsy, bring me three or four more
cups of wine so I'll be good and drunk and can disappear.

Winebringer, even if it is a sin, draw two large jugs of wine
from that cask, and bring it over here!

✲

Everyone who is a true lover of God
will be spared from the world and its wicked ways.
O Sufi, on this precipice, live your life in such a way that if your
foot should slip, angels will pray for your safety
and break your fall.

My mind, heart, soul, and all my possessions
are my ransom for His love.
Who has the right to any of this but He?

O breeze, I beg you, bring me something I can worship,
even if it be only a speck of dust.

This separation has made me thirsty.
Winebringer, more wine! And bring that cup of mirrors too.

O, birds of the woods, be thankful that you are free
and so full of joy. For those captured in cages only sing of grief.

O candyman, bring me some sugar from the Beloved's lip.
My love-disease is tired of so much salt!

✡

Winebringer, bring me a glass of wine that's on fire!
Being here with all these Perfect Masters has made me insecure.

The tale of wine and kisses from the Beloved
has flowed from Hafiz's pen.
But with hand tired and fingers sore,
he wants to know: when will this sad story end?

The Beloved told Hafiz: "Make up your mind!
To reach nirvana is a lofty goal.
To get there, get out that map of Love
and find your way back to Me!"

✲

In the spring when tulips bloom is the time for drinking wine!
Don't be a hypocrite: make friends, too, with roses and the wind.

If it is your dream to be wed to the Great Mystery, then come;
but first be a friend of wine before you go out doing good.

Like the rosebud, the world and its business is closed up tight.
So be like the spring breeze and open up that bud!

Winebringer, don't put off until tomorrow
what you can do today.
Bring me proof from the Book of Life
that my future and my fate are written in blood.

Hafiz says: If it's illusion that you want, go get up on that screen!
You'll find me in Winestreet laughing, drunk on His perfume!

✲

When I asked the Winemaster about the path to Truth,
He told me to keep quiet and took my glass of wine away.

O Beloved, I have tied my trust to the tip of Your long, flowing hair;
why should I do anything else? For without You, I don't exist.

But the beautiful soft cheek of a lover
teaches us how to also love the Friend.
To praise Her beautiful face is praising His face, too.

✡

Today, instead of going to church,
I'm going to the Winehouse to drink some wine.
I don't have time to listen to those jobless preachers
and their empty words.

Hafiz, kiss only the Beloved's lips
and drink only the Beloved's wine.For He is the only reverend,
and His wine is the only sacrament you need!

✲

I said: "O Beloved, look at me, I am healthy and prosperous.
When will I get Your kiss?
And how do I avoid idiots and idols along the way?"

He said: "In the Street of Love there are those who tell stories,
and there are those who tell the truth."

I said: "What do wine and all the preacher's robes
have to do with religion?"
He said: "This is like kindergarten to get into the Master's school."

I said: "And when will we see this kind Master
standing at our door?"
He said: "Not until Jupiter collides with the moon,
or until you can drink a cask of wine."

✲

In the days when kings were honorable, fair, and forgiving,
professors, priests, and Hafiz all drank from the same cup.

Winebringer, more wine!
Soon it will be spring and there will be no more wine.
Tell me what I should do about my burning heart.

A long time ago, I went to the fortune-teller
to have my fortune read.
She said: "Go to the Winehouse and drink a cup of wine."

Hafiz has been here ever since.
He is through with his love of suffering
and the words that describe that love,
and he's going to stay that way!

✡

O Beloved,
do you think that I've been lying around sleeping all these years?
Or that I've learned to be patient from all this separation
and all this pain? Lord, no!

To be cut wide open by Your hand is better than another's cure.
Your poison is better than anything the pharmacist prescribes.

Hafiz says: "Who really knows You as You really are?
It's like the blind telling the blind what it is they see.

✡

O Beloved,
tonight I will write my poems from the light of Your face,
rather than from the moonlit sky.

The face of the Beloved can only be seen by those who are pure,
so don't waste your time looking
unless your mirror is completely clean.

Hafiz says: "O, pilgrim, give up your religion.
Love is a mystery, and like light upon your face, it plays.

✡

O Beloved,
I know my ghazals are not always loving and worthy of You.
I promise, from now on, I'll only sing You perfect songs.

Oh no! The wind has stopped blowing.
How, now, will my ghazals or my words ever get to You?

O Beloved, where are you? Since You left,
my heart has become a fountain,
and blood is pouring from my eyes.

From the root of every eyelash trickles a hundred drips of blood,
and from my heart pour gallons more!

Hafiz has become a slave to this grieving. In the winecup
he can see his past, and he thinks about it night and day.

☆

If I happen to make it over to Your street,
I would consider myself blessed to share with You my poems.

Because the jewel of Your love has given polish to my heart,
it's also clean of the rust of trouble and defeat.

My life will only be complete after I have lost it
to misfortune and given my desires away.

This is Hafiz, and I am standing at Your door.
Where else is there for me to go?

I am the King of Hearts, ask anyone.
No one has suffered this much pain!

Here...here are Hafiz's poems.
They are proof of my devotion and my love.
I offer them in silence, and they're all I've got to say.

✡

The Author
&
The Translator

Persian lyric poet Hafiz (born Khwaāja Šamsu d-Dīn Muhammad Hāfez-e Šīrāzī) grew up in Shiraz. Very little is known about his life, but it is thought that he may have memorized the *Qur'an* after hearing his father recite passages. When his father died, he left school to work at a bakery and as a copyist. Hafiz became a poet at the court of Abu Ishak and also taught at a religious college. He is one of the most celebrated of the Persian poets, and his influence can be felt to this day. As the author of numerous ghazals expressing love, spirituality, and protest, he and his work continue to be important to Iranians, and many of his poems are used as proverbs or sayings.

Thomas Rain Crowe is an internationally-published and recognized author, editor and translator of more than thirty books, including the multi-award winning nonfiction nature memoir *Zoro's Field: My Life in the Appalachian Woods* (University of Georgia Press, 2005); an internationally acclaimed anthology of contemporary Celtic language poets entitled *Writing the Wind: A Celtic Resurgence* (The New Celtic Poetry); his collection of poetry *The Laugharne Poems* (Gwasg Carreg Gwalch; Wales) written at the Dylan Thomas boathouse in Laugharne, Wales in 1993 and 1995, and *The Book of Rocks* (Les Aretes; France, 2008). He has translated two volumes of the poetry of the Sufi poet Hafiz—*In Wineseller's Street* (Ibex/Iran Books) and *Drunk On the Wine of the Beloved* (Shambhala Publications) as well as *Painting From the Palette of Love: The Mystical Poetry of Kabir* (Shambhala Publications). He has been an editor of major literary and cultural journals and anthologies and is founder and publisher of New Native Press. He lived in San Francisco during the 1970s working alongside all the people cited in his book *Starting From San Francisco: Beats, Baby Beats & The 1970s San Francisco Renaissance* (Third Mind Books, 2018). His most recent book is *New Natives: Becoming Indigenous in a Time of Crisis and Transition* (Iris Press, 2025). He lives in the Great Smoky Mountains of North Carolina.

Praise for Thomas Rain Crow's Translations

"Thomas Rain Crowe has done a masterful job bringing out the spirit of Hafiz's romantic longing, which is in truth, a deep spiritual yearning for the Beloved, an original longing, or original love for All There Is. Hafiz understands that this original source of love will always remain a Great Mystery. Crowe renders his words this way: 'The face of the Beloved can only be seen by those who are pure, so don't waste your time looking unless your mirror is completely clean,' Hafiz says: 'O pilgrim, give up your religion. Love is a mystery, and like light upon your face, it plays.' I am grateful for this rendering of the best of Hafiz' *Divan*. *Dancing with the Beloved* is a way-shower to remembering the Divine."

—Glenn Aparicio Parry,
author of *Original Love: The Timeless Source of Wholeness* and the Nautilus award-winning *Original Thinking: A Radical ReVisionng of Time, Humanity, and Nature*

"Hafiz was drunk with the divine wine. What an intoxication he had! The wine of grapes could not compete with Hafiz and his intoxicating 'brew.' Only a man who was spiritually 'drunk' all the time could write such stanzas that can make you drunk too. We must do as he said and wake up the beauty and glory of our home here in our hearts. With pen and paper, Crowe is letting the world know it."

—Irwin Luck
Author of *The Silent Master Meher Baba*

"What Robert Bly did to Kabir and what Coleman Barks did to Rumi, Thomas Rain Crowe has done to the mystical poetry of Hafiz—-made it fresh, contemporary, and accessible. "

—Ramesh Bjonnes,
author of *Sacred Body, Sacred Spirit*

"Thomas Crowe brings the voice of Hafiz alive for us today. It feels as if the poet were speaking from the steps of a local tavern. Blunt, direct, funny, ecstatic, and so very human, these poems call us to join him in the arms of the Beloved.

—Rick Hanson, Ph.D.,
author of *Buddha's Brain, Hardwiring Happiness, and Resilience*

"Like Hafiz drunk on God in the Winehouse, it was wonderful to read *Dancing With the Beloved*! Along with Hafiz's signature humor and contemporary relevance, Crowe's translations echo Kabir's irreverence and ecstatic love, and Rumi's longing for the Beloved— good medicine for our time praising security through cryptocurrency and salvation through AI. Hafiz warned, 'Pilgrim, put down that book you are reading/about money and the rich.' This book is full of gems for seekers, writers, and others, in many cases desperate for meaning through external recognition,.. 'like a loud voice that the Winebringer hears / over all his other customers.' If I were still teaching poetry, I would use this book."

—Scott T. Starbuck,
author of *Hawk on Wire* and *Bridge at the End of the World*

Companions for the Journey Series

Inspirational work by well-known writers in a small-book format designed to be carried along on your journey through life.

Volume 33
Dancing with the Beloved
Hafiz
Translated by Thomas Rain Crowe
978-1-945680-92-2 88 pages

Volume 32
Songs of Mirabai
Translated by Andrew Schelling
978-1-945680-78-6 137 pages

Volume 31
Homage to Green Tea
Ch'oŭi
Translated by Ian Haight & T'ae-yŏng Hŏ
978-1-945680-71-7 109 pages

Volume 30
Returning Home: The Poetry of Tao Yuan-ming
Translated by Dan Veach
978-1-945680-69-4 118 pages

Volume 29

Taken to Heart: 70 Poems from the Chinese

Translated by Gary Young and Yanwen Xu

978-1-945680-58-8 104 pages

Volume 28

Dreaming of Fallen Blossoms

Tune Poems of Su Dong-Po

Translated by Yun Wang

978-1-945680-27-4 243 pages

Volume 27

Precious Mirror

Kobun Otogawa

Translated by Gary Young

978-1-945680-21-1 100 pages

Volume 26

Unexpected Development

Klaus Merz

Translated by Marc Vincenz

978-1-945680-14-4 142 pages

Volume 25

A House by Itself

Selected Haiku: Masaoka Shiki

Translated by John Brandi & Noriko Kawasaki Martinez

978-1-945680-09-0 102 pages

Volume 24

Poetics of Wonder: Passage to Mogador

Alberto Ruy-Sanchez

Translated by Rhonda Dahl Buchanan

978-1-935210-55-9   156 pages

Volume 23

Searching for Guan Yin

Sarah E. Truman

978-1-935210-28-3   288 pages

Volume 22

Finding the Way Home

Poems of Awakening and Transformation

Edited by Dennis Maloney

978-1-935210-12-2   190 pages

Volume 21

What Happened Was . . .

On Writing Personal Essay and Memoir

Genie Zeiger

978-935210-04-7   106 pages

Volume 20

Mountain Tasting: Haiku and Journals of Santoka Taneda

Translated by John Stevens

978-1-935210-03-0   200 pages

Volume 19

Between the Floating Mist

Poems of Ryokan

Translated by Hide Oshiro and Dennis Maloney

978-1-935210-05-4 90 pages

Volume 18

Breaking the Willow:

Poems of Parting, Exile, Separation and Return

Translated by David Lunde

978-1-893996-95-3 96 pages

Volume 17

The Secret Gardens of Mogador

A Novel by Alberto Ruy-Sanchez

Translated by Rhonda Dahl Buchanan

978-1-893996-99-1 240 pages

Volume 16

Majestic Nights

Love Poems of Bengali Women

Translated by Carolyne Wright and co-translators

978-1-893996-93-9 108 pages

Volume 15

Dropping the Bow

Poems from Ancient India

Translated by Andrew Schelling

978-1-893996-96-0 128 pages

Volume 14

White Crane

Love Songs of the Sixth Dali Lama

Translated by Geoffrey R. Waters

1-893996-82-4 86 pages

Volume 13

Haiku Master Buson

Translated by Edith Shiffert and Yuki Sawa

1-893996-81-6 256 pages

Volume 12

The Shape of Light

Prose Pieces by James Wright

1-893996-85-9 96 pages

Volume 11

Simmering Away: Songs from the Kanginshu

Translated by Yasuhiko Moriguchi and David Jenkins

Illustrations by Michael Hofmann

1-893996-49-2 70 pages

Volume 10

Because of the Rain: Korean Zen Poems

Translated by Won-Chung Kim and Christopher Merrill

1-893996-44-1 96 pages

Volume 9

Pilgrim of the Clouds

Poems and Essays from Ming Dynasty China

Translated by Jonathan Chaves

1-893996-39-5 192 pages

Volume 8

The Unswept Path: Contemporary American Haiku

Edited by John Brandi and Dennis Maloney.

1-893996-38-7 220 pages

Volume 7

Lotus Moon: The Poetry of Rengetsu

Translated by John Stevens

Afterword by Bonnie Myotai Treace

893996-36-0 132 pages

Volume 6

A Zen Forest: Zen Sayings

Translated by Soioku Shigematsu

Preface by Gary Snyder

1-893996-30-1 120 pages

Volume 5

Back Roads to Far Towns

Basho's Travel Journal

Translated by Cid Corman

1-893996-31-X 94 pages

Volume 4

Heaven My Blanket, Earth My Pillow

Poems from Sung Dynasty China by Yang Wan-Li

Translated by Jonathan Chaves

I-893996-29-8 288 pages

Volume 3

10,000 Dawns: The Love Poems of Claire and Yvan Goll

Translated by Thomas Rain Crowe and Nan Watkins

I-893996-27-I. 88 pages

Volume 2

There Is No Road: Proverbs by Antonio Machado

Translated by Mary G. Berg and Dennis Maloney

I-893996-66-2 118 pages

Volume I

Wild Ways: Zen Poems of Ikkyu

Translated by John Stevens

I-893996-65-4 152 pages